George Meredith

Odes

In Contribution to the Song of French History

George Meredith

Odes

In Contribution to the Song of French History

ISBN/EAN: 9783337180706

Printed in Europe, USA, Canada, Australia, Japan

Cover: Foto ©ninafisch / pixelio.de

More available books at **www.hansebooks.com**

ODES

IN CONTRIBUTION
TO THE SONG
OF FRENCH
HISTORY

BY

GEORGE MEREDITH

WESTMINSTER

ARCHIBALD CONSTABLE AND CO

2 WHITEHALL GARDENS

1898

BUTLER & TANNER,
THE SELWOOD PRINTING WORKS,
FROME, AND LONDON.

INSCRIBED TO THE

RIGHT HON. JOHN MORLEY, M.P.

CONTENTS

THE REVOLUTION

B

THE REVOLUTION

NOT yet had History's Ætna smoked the skies,
And low the Gallic Giantess lay enchained,
While overhead in ordered set and rise,
Her kingly crowns immutably defiled ;
Effulgent on funereal piled
Across the vacant heavens, and distrained
Her body, mutely, even as earth, to bear ;
Despoiled the tomb of hope, her mouth of air.

Through marching scores of winters racked she lay,
Beneath a hoar-frost's brilliant crust;
Whereon the jewelled flies that drained
Her breasts disported in a glistering spray ;
She, the land's fount of fruits, enclosed with dust ;
By good and evil angels fed, sustained
In part to curse, in part to pray,

Sucking the dubious rumours, till men saw
The throbs of her charged heart before the Just,
So worn the harrowed surface had become:
And still they deemed the dance above was Law,
Amort all passion in a rebel dumb.

III

Then on the unanticipated day,
Earth heaved, and rose a veinous mound
To roar of the underfloods; and off it sprang,
Ravishing as red wine in woman's form,
A splendid Mænad, she of the delirious laugh,
Her body twisted flames with the smoke-cap crowned;
She of the Bacchic foot; the challenger to the fray,
Bewitchment for the embrace; who sang, who sang
Intoxication to her swarm,
Revolved them, hair, voice, feet, in her carmagnole,
As with a stroke she snapped the Royal staff
Dealt the awaited blow on gilt decay
(O ripeness of the time! O Retribution sure,
If but our vital lamp illume us to endure!)
And, like a glad releasing of her soul,
Sent the word Liberty up to meet the midway blue,
Her bridegroom in descent to her; and they joined,
In the face of men they joined: attest it true,
The million witnesses, that she

For ages lying beside the mole,
Was on the unanticipated miracle day
Upraised to midway heaven and, as to her goal
Enfolded, ere the Immaculate knew
What Lucifer of the Mint had coined
His bride's adulterate currency
Of burning love corrupt of an infuriate hate ;
She worthy, she unworthy; that one day his mate :
His mate for that one day of the unwritten deed.
Read backward on the hoar-frost's brilliant crust ;
Beneath it read.
Athirst to kiss, athirst to slay, she stood,
A radiance fringed with grim affright ;
For them that hungered, she was nourishing food,
For those who sparkled, Night.
Read in her heart, and how before the Just
Her doings, her misdoings, plead.

IV

Down on her leap for him the young Angelical broke
To husband a resurgent France :
From whom, with her dethroning stroke,
Dishonour passed ; the dalliance,
That is occasion's yea or nay,
In issues for the soul to pay,
Discarded ; and the cleft 'twixt deed and word,

The sinuous lie which warbles the sweet bird,
Wherein we see old Darkness peer,
Cold Dissolution beck, she had flung hence ;
And hence the talons and the beak of prey ;
Hence all the lures to silken swine
Thronging the troughs of indolence ;
With every sleek convolvement serpentine ;
The pride in elfin arts to veil an evil leer,
And bid a goatfoot trip it like a fay.
He clasped in this revived, uprisen France,
A valorous dame, of countenance
The lightning's upon cloud : unlit as yet
On brows and lips the lurid shine
Of seas in the night-wind's whirl ; unstirred
Her pouch of the centuries' injuries compressed ;
The shriek that tore the world as yet unheard :
Earth's animate full flower she looked, intense
For worship, wholly given him, fair
Adoring or desiring ; in her bright jet,
Earth's crystal spring to sky : Earth's warrior Best
To win Heaven's Pure up that midway
We vision for new ground, where sense
And spirit are one for the further flight ; breast-bare,
Bare-limbed ; nor graceless gleamed her disarray
In scorn of the seductive insincere,
But martially nude for hot Bellona's play,
And amorous of the loftiest in her view.

V

She sprang from dust to drink of earth's cool dew,
The breath of swaying grasses share,
Mankind embrace, their weaklings rear,
At wrestle with the tyrannic strong;
Her forehead clear to her mate, virgin anew,
As immortals may be in the mortal sphere.
Read through her launching heart, who had lain long
With Earth and heard till it became her own,
Our good Great Mother's eve and matin song:
The humming burden of Earth's toil to feed
Her creatures all, her task to speed their growth,
Her aim to lead them up her pathways, shown
Between the Pains and Pleasures; warned of both,
Of either aided on their hard ascent.
Now when she looked with love's benign delight
After great ecstasy, along the plains,
What foulest impregnation of her sight
Transformed the scene to multitudinous troops
Of human sketches, quaver-figures, bent,
As were they winter sedges, broken hoops,
Dry udders, vineless poles, worm-eaten posts,
With features like the flowers defaced by deluge rains?
Recked she that some perverting devil had limned
Earth's proudest to spout scorn of the Maker's hand,
Who could a day behold these deathly hosts.

And see, decked, graced, and delicately trimmed
A ribanded and gemmed elected few,
Sanctioned, of milk and honey starve the land:—
Like melody in flesh, its pleasant game
Olympianwise perform, cloak but the shame:
Beautiful statures; hideous,
By Christian contrast; pranked with golden chains,
And flexile where is manhood straight;
Mortuaries where warm should beat
The brotherhood that keeps blood sweet:
Who dared in cantique impious,
Proclaim the Just, to whom was due
Cathedral gratitude in the pomp of state,
For that on those lean outcasts hung the sucker Pains,
On these elect the swelling Pleasures grew.
Surely a devil's land when that meant death for each!
Fresh from the breast of Earth, not thus,
With all the body's life to plump the leech,
Is Nature's way, she knew. The abominable scene
Spat at the skies; and through her veins,
To cloud celestially sown,
Ran venom of what nourishment
Her dark sustainer subterrene
Supplied her, stretched supine on the rack,
Alive in the shrewd nerves, the seething brains,
Under derisive revels, prone
As one clamped fast, with the interminable senseless
    blent.

VI

Now was her face white waves in the tempest's sharp ?
  flame-blink ;
Her skies shot black.
Now was it visioned infamy to drink
Of earth's cool dew, and through the vines
Frolic in pearly laughter with her young,
Watching the healthful, natural, happy signs
Where hands of lads and maids like tendrils clung,
After their sly shy ventures from the leaf,
And promised bunches. Now it seemed
The world was one malarious mire,
Crying for purification : chief
This land of France. It seemed
A duteous desire
To drink of life's hot flood, and the crimson streamed.

VII

She drank what makes man demon at the draught.
Her skies lowered black,
Her lover flew,
There swept a shudder over men.
Her heavenly lover fled her, and she laughed,
For laughter was her spirit's weapon then.
The Infernal rose uncalled, he with his crew.

VIII

As mighty thews burst manacles, she went mad :
Her heart a flaring torch usurped her wits.
Such enemies of her next-drawn breath she had!
To tread her down in her live grave beneath
Their dancing floor sunned blind by the Royal wreath,
They ringed her steps with crafty prison pits.
Without they girdled her, made nest within.
There ramped the lion, here entrailed the snake.
They forced the cup to her lips when she drank blood ;
Believing it, in the mother's mind at strain,
In the mother's fears, and in young Liberty's wail
Alarmed, for her encompassed children's sake ;
The sole sure way to save her priceless bud.
Wherewith, when power had gifted her to prevail,
Vengeance appeared as logically akin.
Insanely rational they ; she rationally insane ;
And in compute of sin, was hers the appealing sin.

IX

Amid the plash of scarlet mud
Stained at the mouth, drunk with our common air,
Not lack of love was her defect ;
The Fury mourned and raged and bled for France ;
Breathing from exultation to despair
At every wild-winged hope struck by mischance

Soaring at each faint gleam o'er her abyss.
Heard still, to be heard while France shall stand erect,
The frontier march she piped her sons, for where
Her crouching outer enemy camped,
Attendant on the deadlier inner's hiss.
She piped her sons the frontier march, the wine
Of martial music, History's cherished tune;
And they, the saintliest labourers that aye
Dropped sweat on soil for bread, took arms and
    tramped;
High-breasted to match men or elements,
Or Fortune, harsh schoolmistress with the undrilled:
War's ragged pupils; many a wavering line,
Torn from the dear fat soil of champaigns hopefully
    tilled,
Torn from the motherly bowl, the homely spoon,
To jest at famine, ply
The novel scythe, and stand to it on the field;
Lie in the furrows, rain-clouds for their tents;
Fronting the red artillery straighten spine;
Buckle the shiver at sight of comrades strewn;
Over an empty platter affect the merrily filled;
Die, if the multiple hazards around said die;
Downward measure a foeman mightily sized;
Laugh at the legs that would run for a life despised;
Lyrical on into death's red roaring jaw-gape, steeled
Gaily to take of the foe his lesson, and give reply.
Cheerful apprentices, they shall be masters soon!

X ✓

Lo, where hurricane flocks of the North-wind rattle
their thunder
Loud through a night, and at dawn comes change to
the great South-west,
Hounds are the hounded in clouds, waves, forests, in-
verted the race :
Lo, in the day's young beams the colossal invading
pursuers
Burst upon rocks and were foam ;
Ridged up a torrent crest ;
Crumbled to ruin, still gazing a glacial wonder ;
Turned shamed feet toe to heel on their track at a
panic pace.
Yesterday's clarion cock scudded hen of the invalid
comb ;
They, the triumphant tonant towering upper, were
under ;
They, violators of home, dared hope an inviolate home ;
They that had stood for the stroke were the vigorous
hewers ;
Quick as the trick of the wrist with the rapier, they
the pursuers.
Heavens and men amazed heard the arrogant crying
for grace ;
Saw the once hearth-reek rabble the scourge of an
army dispieced ;

Saw such a shift of the hunt as when Titan Olympus
    clomb.
Fly! was the sportsman's word; and the note of the
    quarry rang, Chase!

XI

Banners from South, from East,
Sheaves of pale banners drooping hole and shred;
The captive brides of valour, Sabine Wives
Plucked from the foeman's blushful bed,
For glorious muted battle-tongues
Of deeds along the horizon's red,
At cost of unreluctant lives;
Her toilful heroes homeward poured,
To give their fevered mother air of the lungs.
She breathed, and in the breathing craved.
Environed as she was, at bay,
Safety she kissed on her drawn sword,
And waved for victory, for fresh victory waved:
She craved for victory as her daily bread;
For victory as her daily banquet raved.

XII

Now had her glut of vengeance left her grey
Of blood, who in her entrails fiercely tore

To clutch and squeeze her snakes; herself the more
Devitalizing: red was her Auroral ray;
Desired if but to paint her pallid hue.
The passion for that young horizon red,
Which dowered her with the flags, the blazing fame,
Like dotage of the past-meridian dame
For some bright Sungod adolescent, swelled
Insatiate, to the voracious grew,
The glutton's inward raveners bred;
Till she, mankind's most dreaded, most abhorred,
Witless in her demands on Fortune, asked,
As by the weaving Fates impelled,
To have the thing most loathed, the iron lord,
Controller and chastiser, under Victory masked.

XIII

Banners from East, from South.
She hugged him in them, feared the scourge they
    meant,
Yet blindly hugged, and hungering built his throne.
So may you see the village innocent,
With curtsey of shut lids and open mouth.
In act to beg for sweets expect a loathly stone:
See furthermore the Just in his measures weigh
Her sufferings and her sins, dispense her meed.
False to her bridegroom lord of the miracle day,
She fell: from his ethereal home observed
Through love, grown alien love, not moved to plead

Against the season's fruit for deadly Seed,
But marking how she had aimed, and where she
    swerved,
Why suffered, with a sad consenting thought.
Nor would he shun her sullen look, nor monstrous hold
The doer of the monstrous ; she aroused,
She, the long tortured, suddenly freed, distraught,
More strongly the divine in him than when
Joy of her as she sprang from mould
Drew him the midway heavens adown
To clasp her in his arms espoused
Before the sight of wondering men,
And put upon the day a deathless crown.
The veins and arteries of her, fold in fold,
His alien love laid open, to divide
The martyred creature from her crimes ; he knew
What cowardice in her valour could reside ;
What strength her weakness covered ; what abased
Sublimity so illumining, and what raised
This wallower in old slime to noblest heights,
Up to the union on the midway blue :—
Day that the celestial grave Recorder hangs
Among dark History's nocturnal lights,
With vivid beams indicative to the quick
Of all who have felt the vaulted body's pangs
Beneath a mind in hopeless soaring sick.
She had forgot how, long enslaved, she yearned
To the one helping hand above ;

Forgot her faith in the Great Undiscerned,
Whereof she sprang aloft to her Angelical love
That day : and he, the bright day's husband, still with
    love,
Though alien, though to an upper seat retired,
Beheld a wrangling heart, as 'twere her soul
On eddies of wild waters cast ;
In wilderness division ; fired
For domination, freedom, lust,
The Pleasures ; lo, a witch's snaky bowl
Set at her lips ; the blood-drinker's madness fast
Upon her ; and therewith mistrust,
Most of herself : a mouth of guile.
Compassionately could he smile,
To hear the mouth disclaiming God,
And clamouring for the Just !
Her thousand impulses, like torches, coursed
City and field ; and pushed abroad
O'er hungry waves to thirsty sands,
Flaring at further ; she had grown to be
The headless with the fearful hands ;
To slaughter, else to suicide enforced.
But he, remembering how his love began,
And of what creature, pitied when was plain
Another measure of captivity
The need for strap and rod :
The penitential prayers again ;
Again the bitter bowing down to dust ;

The burden on the flesh for who disclaims the God
The answer when is call upon the Just.
Whence her lost virtue had found refuge strode
Her Master, saying, " I only; I who can! "
And echoed round her army, now her chain.
So learns the nation closing Anarch's reign,
That she has been in travail of a Man.

NAPOLÉON

.

NAPOLÉON

CANNON his name,
Cannon his voice, he came.
Who heard of him heard shaken hills,
An earth at quake, to quiet stamped ;
Who looked on him beheld the will of wills,
The driver of wild flocks where lions ramped :
Beheld War's liveries flee him, like lumped grass
Nid-nod to ground beneath the cuffing storm ;
While laurelled over his Imperial form,
Forth from her bearded tube of lacquey brass,
Reverberant notes and long blew volant Fame.
Incarnate Victory, Power manifest,
Infernal or God-given to mankind,
On the quenched volcano's cusp did he take stand,
A conquering army's height above the land,
Which calls that army offspring of its breast,
And sees it mid the starry camps enshrined ;
His eye the cannon's flame,
The cannon's cave his mind.

II

To weld the nation in a name of dread,
And scatter carrion flies off wounds unhealed,
The Necessitated came, as comes from out
Electric ebon lightning's javelin-head,
Threatening annihilation in the revealed
Founts of our being ; terrible with doubt,
With radiance restorative. At one stride
Athwart the Law he stood for sovereign sway.
That Soliform made featureless beside
His brilliancy who neighboured : vapour they ;
Vapour what postured statutes barred his tread.
On high in amphitheatre field on field,
Italian, Egyptian, Austrian,
Far heard and of the carnage discord clear,
Bells of his escalading triumphs pealed
In crashes on a choral chant severe,
Heraldic of the authentic Charlemagne,
Globe, sceptre, sword, to enfold, to rule, to smite,
Make unity of the mass,
Coherent or refractory, by his might.

Forth from her bearded tube of lacquey brass,
Fame blew, and tuned the jangles, bent the knees
Rebellious or submissive ; his decrees
Were thunder in those heavens and compelled :

Such as disordered earth, eclipsed of stars,
Endures for sign of Order's calm return,
Whereunto she is vowed ; and his wreckage-spars,
His harried ships, old riotous Ocean lifts alight,
Subdued to splendour in his delirant churn.
Glory suffused the accordant, quelled,
By magic of high sovereignty, revolt :
And he, the reader of men, himself unread ;
The name of hope, the name of dread ;
Bloom of the coming years or blight ;
An arm to hurl the bolt
With aim Olympian ; bore
Likeness to Godhead. Whither his flashes hied
Hosts fell ; what he constructed held rock-fast.
So did earth's abjects deem of him that built and clove.
Torch on imagination, beams he cast,
Whereat they hailed him deified :
If less than an eagle-speeding Jove, than Vulcan more.
Or it might be a Vulcan-Jove,
Europe for smithy, Europe's floor
Lurid with sparks in evanescent showers,
Loud echo-clap of hammers at all hours,
Our skies the reflex of its furnace blast.

III

On him the long enchained, released
For bride of the miracle day up the midway blue ;

She from her heavenly lover fallen to serve for feast
Of rancours and raw hungers ; she, the untrue,
Yet pitiable, not despicable, gazed.
Fawning her body bent, she gazed
With eyes the moonstone portals to her heart :
Eyes magnifying through hysteric tears
This apparition, ghostly for belief ;
Demoniac or divine, but sole
Over earth's mightiest written Chief ;
Earth's chosen, crowned, unchallengeable upstart :
The trumpet word to awake, transform, renew ;
The arbiter of circumstance ;
High above limitations, as the spheres.
Nor ever had heroical Romance,
Never ensanguined History's lengthened scroll,
Shown fulminant to shoot the levin dart
Terrific as this man, by whom upraised,
Aggrandized and begemmed, she outstripped her
    peers ;
Like midnight's levying brazier-beacon blazed
Defiant to the world, a rally for her sons,
Day of the darkness ; this man's mate ; by him,
Cannon his name,
Rescued from vivisectionist and knave,
Her body's dominators and her shame ;
By him with the rivers of ranked battalions, brave
Past mortal, girt : a march of swords and guns
Incessant ; his proved warriors ; loaded dice

He flung on the crested board, where chilly Fears
Behold the Reaper's ground, Death sitting grim,
Awatch for his predestined ones,
Mid shrieks and torrent-hooves ; but these,
Inebriate of his inevitable device,
Hail it their hero's wood of lustrous laurel-trees,
Blossom and fruit of fresh Hesperides,
The boiling life-blood in their cheers.
Unequalled since the world was man they pour
A spiky girdle round her ; these, her sons,
His cataracts at smooth holiday, soon to roar
Obstruction shattered at his will or whim :
Kind to her ear as quiring Cherubim,
And trampling earth like scornful mastodons.

IV

The flood that swept her to be slave
Adoring, under thought of being his mate,
These were, and unto the visibly unexcelled,
As much of heart as abjects can she gave,
Or what of heart the body bears for freight
When Majesty apparent overawes ;
By the flash of his ascending deeds upheld,
Which let not feminine pride in him have pause
To question where the nobler pride rebelled.
She read the hieroglyphic on his brow,
Felt his firm hand to wield the giant's mace ;

Herself whirled upward in an eagle's claws,
Past recollection of her earthly place ;
And if cold Reason pressed her, called him Fate ;
Offering abashed the servile woman's vow.
Delirium was her virtue when the look
At fettered wrists and violated laws
Faith in a rectitude Supernal shook,
Till worship of him shone as her last rational state,
The slave's apology for gemmed disgrace.
Far in her mind that leap from earth to the ghost
Midway on high ; or felt as a troubled pool ;
Or as a broken sleep that hunts a dream half lost,
Arrested and rebuked by the common school
Of daily things for truancy. She could rejoice
To know with wakeful eyeballs Violence
Her crowned possessor, and, on every sense
Incumbent, Fact, Imperial Fact, her choice,
In scorn of barren visions, aims at a glassy void.
Who sprang for Liberty once, found slavery sweet ;
And Tyranny on alert subservience buoyed,
Spurred a blood-mare immeasurably fleet
To shoot the transient leagues in a passing wink,
Prompt for the glorious bound at the fanged abyss's
        brink.
Scarce felt she that she bled when battle scored
On riddled flags the further conjured line ;
From off the meteor gleam of his waved sword
Reflected bright in permanence : she bled

As the Bacchante spills her challengeing wine
With whirl o' the cup before the kiss to lip ;
And bade drudge History in his footprints tread,
For pride of sword-strokes o'er slow penmanship :
Each step of his a volume : his sharp word
The shower of steel and lead
Or pastoral sunshine

V

Persistent through the brazen chorus round
His thunderous footsteps on the foeman's ground,
A broken carol of wild notes was heard,
As when an ailing infant wails a dream.
Strange in familiarity it rang :
And now along the dark blue vault might seem
Winged migratories having but heaven for home,
Now the lone sea-bird's cry down shocks of foam,
Beneath a ruthless paw the captive's pang.

It sang the gift that comes from God
To mind of man as air to lung.
So through her days of under sod
Her faith unto her heart had sung,
Like bedded seed by frozen clod,
With view of wide-armed heaven and buds at burst
And midway up, Earth's fluttering little lyre.
Even for a glimpse, for even a hope in chained desire
The vision of it watered thirst.

VI

But whom those errant moans accused
As Liberty's murderous mother, cried accursed,
France blew to deafness : for a space she mused ;
She smoothed a startled look, and sought,
From treasuries of the adoring slave,
Her surest way to strangle thought ;
Picturing her dread lord decree advance
Into the enemy's land ; artillery, bayonet, lance ;
His ordering fingers point the dial's to time their
    ranks :
Himself the black storm-cloud, the tempest's bayonet-
    glaive.
Like foam-heads of a loosened freshet bursting banks,
By mount and fort they thread to swamp the slug-
    gard plains.
Shines his gold-laurel sun, or cloak connivent rains.
They press to where the hosts in line and square
    throng mute ;
He watchful of their form, the Audacious, the Astute ;
Eagle to grip the field ; to work his craftiest, fox.
From his brief signal, straight the stroke of the leveller
    falls ;
From him those opal puffs, those arcs with the clouded
    balls :
He waves, and the voluble scene is a quagmire shift-
    ing blocks ;

They clash, they are knotted, and now 'tis the deed
of the axe on the log ;
Here away moves a spiky woodland, and yon away
sweep
Rivers of horse torrent-mad to the shock, and the
heap over heap
Right through the troughed black lines turned to
bunches or shreds, or a fog
Rolling off sunlight's arrows. Not mightier Phoebus
in ire,
Nor deadlier Jove's avengeing right hand, than he of
the brain
Keen at an enemy's mind to encircle and pierce and
constrain,
Muffling his own for a fate-charged blow very Gods
may admire.
Sure to behold are his eagles on high where the con-
flict raged.
Rightly, then, should France worship, and deafen the
disaccord
Of those who dare withstand an irresistible sword
To thwart his predestined subjection of Europe. Let
them submit !
She said it aloud, and heard in her breast, as a singer
caged,
With the beat of wings at bars, Earth's fluttering
little lyre.
No more at midway heaven, but liker midway to the pit :

Not singing the spirally upward of rapture, the down-
    ward of pain
Rather, the drop sheer downward from pressure of
    merciless weight.

Her strangled thought got breath, with her worship
    held debate ;
To yield and sink, yet eye askant the mark she had
    missed.
Over the black-blue rollers of that broad Westerly
    main,
Steady to sky, the light of Liberty glowed
In a flaming pillar, that cast on the troubled waters
    a road
For Europe to cross, and see the thing lost subsist.
For there 'twas a shepherd led his people, no butcher
    of sheep ;
Firmly there the banner he first upreared,
Stands to rally ; and nourishing grain do his children
    reap
From a father beloved in life, in his death revered.
Contemplating him and his work, shall a skyward
    glance
Clearer sight of our dreamed and abandoned ob-
    tain ;
Nay, but as if seen in station above the Republic,
    France
Had view of her one-day's heavenly lover again ;

Saw him amid the bright host looking down on her;
knew she had erred,
Knew him her judge, knew yonder the spirit preferred;
Yonder the base of the summit she strove that day to
ascend,
Ere cannon mastered her soul, and all dreams had end. I

VII

Soon felt she in her shivered frame
, A bodeful drain of blood illume
Her wits with frosty fire to read
The dazzling wizard who would have her bleed
On fruitless marsh and snows of spectral gloom
For victory that was victory scarce in name.
Husky his clarions laboured, and her sighs
O'er slaughtered sons were heavier than the prize;
Recalling how he stood by Frederic's tomb,
With Frederic's country underfoot and spurned:
There meditated; till her hope might guess,
Albeit his constant star prescribe success,
The savage strife would sink, the civil aim
To head a mannered world breathe zephyrous
Of morning after storm; whereunto she yearned;
And Labour's lovely peace, and Beauty's courtly
bloom,
The mind in strenuous tasks hilarious.
At such great height, where hero hero topped,

Right sanely should the Grand Ascendant think
No further leaps at the fanged abyss's brink
True Genius takes : be battle's dice-box dropped !

She watched his desert features, hung to hear
The honey words desired, and veiled her face ;
Hearing the Seaman's name recur
Wrathfully, thick with a meaning worse
Than call to the march : for that inveterate Purse
Could kindle the extinct, inform a vacant place,
Conjure a heart into the trebly felled.
It squeezed the globe, insufferably swelled
To feed insurgent Europe : rear and van
Were haunted by the amphibious curse ;
Here flesh, there phantom, livelier after rout :
The Seaman piping aye to the rightabout,
Distracted Europe's Master, puffed remote
Those Indies of the swift Macedonian,
Whereon would Europe's Master somewhiles doat,
In dreamings on a docile universe
Beneath an immarcessible Charlemagne.

Nor marvel France should veil a seer's face,
And call on darkness as a blest retreat.
Magnanimously could her iron Emperor
Confront submission : hostile stirred to heat
All his vast enginery, allowed no halt
Up withered avenues of waste-blood war,

To the pitiless red mounts of fire afume,
As 'twere the world's arteries opened! Woe the race!
Ask wherefore Fortune's vile caprice should balk
His panther spring across the foaming salt,
From martial sands to the cliffs of pallid chalk!
There is no answer: seed of black defeat
She then did sow, and France nigh unto death fore-
    doom.

See since that Seaman's epicycle sprite
Engirdle, lure and goad him to the chase
Along drear leagues of crimson spotting white
With mother's tears of France, that he may meet
Behind suborned battalions, ranked as wheat
Where peeps the weedy poppy, him of the sea;
Earth's power to baffle Ocean's power resume;
Victorious army crown o'er Victory's fleet;
And bearing low that Seaman upon knee,
Stay the vexed question of supremacy,
Obnoxious in the vault by Frederic's tomb.

VIII

Poured streams of Europe's veins the flood
Full Rhine or Danube rolls off morning-tide
Through shadowed reaches into crimson-dyed:
And Rhine and Danube knew her gush of blood
Down the plucked roots the deepest in her breast.

D

He tossed her cordials, from his laurels pressed.
She drank for dryness thirstily, praised his gifts.
The blooded frame a powerful draught uplifts,
Writhed the devotedness her voice rang wide
In cries ecstatic, as of the martyr-Blest,
Their spirits issuing forth of bodies racked,
And crazy chuckles, with life's tears at feud ;
While near her heart the sunken sentinel
Called Critic marked, and dumb in awe reviewed
This torture, this anointed, this untracked
To mortal source, this alien of his kind ;
Creator, slayer, conjuror, Solon-Mars,
The cataract of the abyss, the star of stars ;
Whose arts to lay the senses under spell
Aroused an insurrectionary mind.

IX

He, did he love her ?　France was his weapon, shrewd
At edge, a wind in onset : he loved well
His tempered weapon, with the which he hewed
Clean to the ground impediments, or hacked,
Sure of the blade that served the great man-miracle.
He raised her, robed her, gemmed her for his bride,
Did but her blood in blindness given exact.
Her blood she gave, was blind to him as guide :
She quivered at his word, and at his touch
Was hound or steed for any mark he espied.

He loved her more than little, less than much.
The fair subservient of Imperial Fact
Next to his consanguineous was placed
In ranked esteem ; above the diurnal meal,
Vexatious carnal appetites above,
Above his hoards, while she Imperial Fact embraced,
And rose but at command from under heel.
The love devolvent, the ascension love,
Receptive or profuse, were fires he lacked,
Whose marrow had expelled their wasteful sparks ;
Whose mind, the vast machine of endless haste,
Took up but solids for its glowing seal.
The hungry love, that fish-like creatures feel,
Impelled for prize of hooks, for prey of sharks,
His night's first quarter sicklied to distaste,
In warm enjoyment barely might distract.
A head that held an Europe half devoured,
Taste in the blood's conceit of pleasure soured.
Nought save his rounding aim, the means he plied,
Death for his cause, to him could point appeal.
His mistress was the thing of uses tried.
Frigid the netting smile on whom he wooed,
But on his Policy his eye was lewd.
That sharp long zig-zag into distance brooked
No foot across ; a shade his ire provoked.
The blunder or the cruelty of a deed,
His Policy imperative could plead.
He deemed nought other precious, nor knew he

Legitimate outside his Policy.
Men's lives and works were due, from their birth's date,
To the State's shield and sword, himself the State.
' He thought for them in mass, as Titan may ;
For their pronounced well-being bade obey ;
O'er each obstructive thicket thunderclapped,
And straight their easy road to market mapped.

Watched Argus to survey the huge preserves
He held or coveted ; Mars was armed alert
At sign of motion ; yet his brows were murk,
His gorge would surge, to see the butcher's work,
The Reaper's field ; a sensitive in nerves.
He rode not over men to do them hurt.
As one who claimed to have for paramour
Earth's fairest form, he dealt the cancelling blow ;
Impassioned, still impersonal ; to ensure
Possession ; free of rivals, not their foe.

The common Tyrant's frenzies, rancour, spites,
He knew as little as men's claim on rights.
A kindness for old servants, early friends,
Was constant in him while they served his ends ;
And if irascible, 'twas the moment's reek
From fires diverted by some gusty freak.
His Policy the act which breeds the act
Prevised, in issues accurately summed
From reckonings of men's tempers, terrors, needs :—

That universal army, which he leads
Who builds Imperial on Imperious Fact.
Within his hot brain's hammering workshop hummed
A thousand furious wheels at whirr, untired
As Nature in her reproductive throes ;
And did they grate, he spake, and cannon fired :
The cause being aye the incendiary foes
Proved by prostration culpable. His dispense
Of Justice made his active conscience ;
His passive was of ceaseless labour formed.
So found this Tyrant sanction and repose ;
Humanly just, inhumanly unwarmed.

Preventive fencings with the foul intent
Occult, by him observed and foiled betimes,
Let fool historians chronicle as crimes.
His blows were dealt to clear the way he went :
Too busy sword and mind for needless blows.
The mighty bird of sky minutest grains
On ground perceived ; in heaven but rays or rains ;
In humankind diversities of masks,
For rule of men the choice of bait or goads.
The statesman steered the despot to large tasks ;
The despot drove the statesman on short roads.
For Order's cause he laboured, as inclined
A soldier's training and his Euclid mind.
His army unto men he could present
As model of the perfect instrument.

That creature, woman, was the sofa soft,
When warriors their dusty armour doffed,
And read their manuals for the making truce
With rosy frailties framed to reproduce.
He farmed his land, distillingly alive
For the utmost extract he might have and hive,
Wherewith to marshal force; and in like scheme,
Benign shone Hymen's torch on young love's
    dream.
Thus to be strong was he beneficent;
A fount of earth, likewise a firmament.

The disputant in words his eye dismayed:
Opinions blocked his passage. Rent
Were Councils with a gesture; brayed
By hoarse camp-phrase what argument
Dared interpose to waken spleen
In him whose vision grasped the unseen,
Whose counsellor was the ready blade,
Whose argument the cannonade.
He loathed his land's divergent parties, loth
To grant them speech, they were such idle troops;
The friable and the grumous, dizzards both.
Men were good sticks his mastery wrought from
    hoops;
Some serviceable, none credible on oath.
The silly preference they nursed to die
In beds he scorned, and led where they should lie.

If magic made them pliable for his use,
Magician he could be by planned surprise.
For do they see the deuce in human guise,
As men's acknowledged head appears the deuce,
And they will toil with devilish craft and zeal.
Among them certain vagrant wits that had
Ideas buzzed ; they were the feebly mad ;
Pursuers of a film they hailed ideal ;
But could be dangerous fire-flies for a brain
Subdued by fact, still amorous of the inane.
With a breath he blew them out, to beat their wings
The way of such transfeminated things,
And France had sense of vacancy in Light.

That is the soul's dead darkness, making clutch
Wild hands for aid at muscles within touch ;
Adding to slavery's chain the stringent twist ;
Even when it brings close surety that aright
She reads her Tyrant through his golden mist ;
Perceives him fast to a harsher Tyrant bound ;
Self-ridden, self-hunted, captive of his aim ;
Material grandeur's ape, the Infernal's hound ;
Enormous, with no infinite around ;
No starred deep sky, no Muse, or lame
The dusty pattering pinions,
The voice as through the brazen tube of Fame.

X

Hugest of engines, a much limited man,
She saw the Lustrous, her great lord, appear
Through that smoked glass her last privation brought
To point her critic eye and spur her thought:
A heart but to propel Leviathan ;
A spirit that breathed but in earth's atmosphere.
Amid the plumed and sceptred ones
Irradiatingly Jovian,
The mountain tower capped by the floating cloud ;
A nursery screamer where dialectics ruled :
Mannerless, graceless, laughterless, unlike
Herself in all, yet with such power to strike,
That she the various features she could scan,
Dared not to sum, though seeing : and befooled
By power which beamed omnipotent, she bowed,
Subservient as roused echo round his guns.
Invulnerable Prince of Myrmidons,
He sparkled, by no sage Athene schooled.
Partly she read her riddle, stricken and pained ;
But irony, her spirit's tongue, restrained.
The Critic, last of vital in the proud
Enslaved, when most detectively endowed,
Admired how irony's venom off him ran,
Like rain-drops down a statue cast in bronze :
Whereby of her keen rapier disarmed,

Again her chant of eulogy began,
Protesting, but with slavish senses charmed.

Her warrior, chief among the valorous great
In arms he was, dispelling shades of blame,
With radiance palpable in fruit and weight.
Heard she reproach, his victories blared response ;
His victories bent the Critic to acclaim,
As with fresh blows upon a ringing sconce.
Or heard she from scarred ranks of jolly growls,
His veterans dwarf their reverence and, like owls,
Laugh in the pitch of discord, to exalt
Their idol for some genial trick or fault,
She, too, became his marching veteran.
Again she took her breath from them who bore
His eagles through the tawny roar,
And murmured at a peaceful state,
That bred the title charlatan,
As missile from the mouth of hate,
For one the daemon fierily filled and hurled,
Cannon his name,
Shattering against a barrier world ;
Her supreme player of man's primaeval game.

The daemon filled him, and he filled her sons ;
Strung them to stature over human height,
As march the standards down the smoky fight ;
Her cherubim, her towering mastodons !

Directed vault or breach, break through
Earth's toughest, seasons, elements, tame ;
Dash at the bulk the sharpened few ;
Count death the smallest of their debts :
Show that the will to do,
Is masculine and begets!

These princes unto him the mother owed ;
These jewels of manhood that rich hand bestowed.
What wonder, though with wits awake
To read her riddle, for these her offspring's sake ;—
And she, before high heaven adulteress,
The lost to honour, in his glory clothed,
Else naked, shamed in sight of men, self-loathed ;—
That she should quench her thought, nor worship less
Than ere she bled on sands or snows and knew
The slave's alternative, to worship or to rue!

XI

Bright from the shell of that much limited man,
Her hero, like the falchion out of sheath,
Like soul that quits the tumbled body, soared :
And France, impulsive, nuptial with his plan,
Albeit the Critic fretting her, adored
Once more. Exultingly her heart went forth,
Submissive to his mind and mood,
The way of those pent-eyebrows North ;

For now was he to win the wreath
Surpassing sunniest in camp or Court ;
Next, as the blessed harvest after years of blight,
Sit, the Great Emperor, to be known the Good !

Now had the Seaman's volvent sprite,
Lean from the chase that barked his contraband,
A beggared applicant at every port,
To strew the profitless deeps and rot beneath,
Slung northward, for a hunted beast's retort
On sovereign power; there his final stand,
Among the perjured Scythian's shaggy horde,
The hydrocephalic aërolite
Had taken; flashing thence repellent teeth,
Though Europe's Master Europe's Rebel banned
To be earth's outcast, ocean's lord and sport.

Unmoved might seem the Master's taunted sword.
Northward his dusky legions nightly slipped,
As on the map of that all-provident head ;
He luting Peace the while, like morning's cock
The quiet day to round the hours for bed ;
No pastoral shepherd sweeter to his flock.
Then Europe first beheld her Titan stripped.
To what vast length of limb and mounds of thews,
How trained to scale the eminences, pluck
The hazards for new footing, how compel
Those timely incidents by men named luck,

Through forethought that defied the Fates to choose
Her grovelling admiration had not yet
Imagined of the great man-miracle ;
And France recounted with her comic smile,
Duplicities of Court and Cabinet,
The silky female of his male in guile,
Wherewith her two-faced Master could amuse
A dupe he charmed in sunny beams to bask,
Before his feint for camisado struck
The lightning moment of the cast-off mask.

Splendours of earth repeating heaven's at set
Of sun down mountain cloud in masses arched ;
Since Asia upon Europe marched,
Unmatched the copious multitudes ; unknown
To Gallia's over-runner, Rome's inveterate foe,
Such hosts ; all one machine for overthrow,
Coruscant from the Master's hand, compact
As reasoned thoughts in the Master's head ; were
　　　shown
Yon lightning moment when his acme might
Blazed o'er the stream that cuts the sandy tract
Borussian from Sarmatia's famished flat ;
The century's flower ; and off its pinnacled throne,
Rayed servitude on Europe's ball of sight.

XII

Behind the Northern curtain-folds he passed.
There heard hushed France her muffled heart beat fast
Against the hollow ear-drum, where she sat
In expectation's darkness, until cracked
The straining curtain-seams : a scaly light
Was ghost above an army under shroud.
Imperious on Imperial Fact
Incestuously the incredible begat.
His veterans and auxiliaries,
The trained, the trustful, sanguine, proud,
Princely, scarce numerable to recite,—
Titanic of all Titan tragedies !—
That Northern curtain took them, as the seas
Gulp the great ships to give back shipmen white.

Alive in marble, she conceived in soul,
With barren eyes and mouth, the mother's loss ;
The bolt from her abandoned heaven sped ;
The snowy army rolling knoll on knoll
Beyond horizon, under no blest Cross :
By the vulture dotted and engarlanded.

Was it a necromancer lured
To weave his tense betraying spell ?
A Titan whom our God endured
Till he of his foul hungers fell,
By all his craft and labour scourged ?

A deluge Europe's liberated wave,
Pæan to sky, leapt over that vast grave.
Its shadow-points against her sacred land converged.
And him, her yoke-fellow, her black lord, her fate,
In doubt, in fevered hope, in chills of hate,
That tore her old credulity to strips,
Then pressed the auspicious relics on her lips,
His withered slave for foregone miracles urged.
And he, whom now his ominous halo's round,
A three parts blank decrescent sickle, crowned,
Prodigious in catastrophe, could wear
The realm of Darkness with its Prince's air;
Assume in mien the resolute pretence
To satiate an hungered confidence,
Proved criminal by the sceptic seen to cower
Beside the generous face of that frail flower.

XIII

Desire and terror then had each of each :
His crown and sword were staked on the magic stroke;
Her blood she gave as one who loved her leech;
And both did barter under union's cloak.
An union in hot fever and fierce need
Of either's aid, distrust in trust did breed.
Their traffic instincts hooded their live wits
To issues. Never human fortune throve
On such alliance. Viewed by fits,

From Vulcan's forge a hovering Jove
Evolved. The slave he dragged the Tyrant drove.
Her awe of him his dread of her invoked :
His nature with her shivering faith ran yoked.
What wisdom counselled, Policy declined ;
All perils dared he save the step behind.
Ahead his grand initiative becked :
One spark of radiance blurred, his orb was wrecked.
Stripped to the despot upstart, for success
He raged to clothe a perilous nakedness.
He would not fall, while falling ; would not be taught,
While learning ; would not relax his grasp on aught
He held in hand, while losing it ; pressed advance,
Pricked for her lees the veins of wasted France ;
Who, had he stayed to husband her, had spun
The strength he taxed unripened for his throw,
In vengeful casts calamitous,
On fields where palsying Pyrrhic laurels grow,
The luminous the ruinous.
An incalescent scorpion,
And fierier for the mounded cirque
That narrowed at him thick and murk,
This gambler with his genius
Flung lives in angry volleys, bloody lightnings, flung
His fortunes to the hosts he stung,
With victories clipped his eagle's wings.
By the hands that built him up was he undone :
By the star aloft, which was his ram's-head will

Within; by the toppling throne the soldier won;
By the yeasty ferment of what once had been,
To cloud a rational mind for present things;
By his own force, the suicide in his mill.
Needs never God of Vengeance intervene
When giants their last lesson have to learn.
Fighting against an end he could discern,
The chivalry whereof he had none,
He called from his worn slave's abundant springs:
Not deigning spousally entreat
That ever blinded by his martial skill,
But harsh to have her worship counted out
In human coin, her vital rivers drained,
Her infant forests felled, commanded die
The decade thousand deaths for his Imperial seat,
Where throning he her faith in him maintained;
Bound Reason to believe delayed defeat
Was triumph; and what strength in her remained
To head against the ultimate foreseen rout,
Insensate taxed; of his impenitent will,
Servant and sycophant: without ally,
In Python's coils, the Master Craftsman still;
The smiter, panther springer, trapper sly,
The deadly wrestler at the crucial bout,
The penetrant, the tonant, tower of towers,
Striking from black disaster starry showers.
Her supreme player of man's primaeval game,
He won his harnessed victim's rapturous shout,

When every move was mortal to her frame,
Her prayer to life that stricken he might lie,
She to exchange his laurels for earth's flowers.

The innumerable whelmed him, and he fell :
A vessel in mid-ocean under storm.
Ere ceased the lullaby of his passing bell,
He sprang to sight, in human form
Revealed, from no celestial aids :
The shades enclosed him, and he fired the shades.

Cannon his name,
Cannon his voice, he came.
The fount of miracles from drought-dust arose,
Amazing even on his Imperial stage,
Where marvels lightened through the alternate hours
And winged o'er human earth's heroical shone.
Into the press of cumulative foes,
Across the friendly fields of smoke and rage,
A broken structure bore his furious powers ;
The man no more, the Warrior Chief the same ;
Match for all rivals ; in himself but flame
Of an outworn lamp, to illumine nought anon.
Yet loud as when he first showed War's effete
Their Schoolman off his eagre mounted high,
And summoned to subject who dared compete,
The cannon in the name Napoleon
Discoursed of sulphur earth to curtained sky.

E

So through a tropic day a regnant sun,
Where armies of assailant vapours thronged,
His glory's trappings laid on them : comes night,
Enwraps him in a bosom quick of heat
From his anterior splendours, and shall seem
Day instant, Day's own lord in the furnace gleam,
The virulent quiver on ravished eyes prolonged,
When severed darkness, all flaminical bright,
Slips vivid eagles linked in rapid flight ;
Which bring at whiles the lionly far roar,
As wrestled he with manacles and gags,
To speed across a cowering world once more,
Superb in ordered floods, his lordly flags.
His name on silence thundered, on the obscure
Lightened ; it haunted morn and even-song :
Earth of her prodigy's extinction long,
With shudderings and with thrillings, hung unsure.

Snapped was the chord that made the resonant bow,
In France, abased and like a shrunken corse ;
Amid the weakest weak, the lowest low,.
From the highest fallen, stagnant off her source ;
Condemned to hear the nations' hostile mirth ;
See curtained heavens, and smell a sulphurous earth ;
Which told how evermore shall tyrant Force
Beget the greater for its overthrow.
The song of Liberty in her hearing spoke
A foreign tongue ; Earth's fluttering little lyre

Unlike, but like the raven's ravening croak.
Not till her breath of being could aspire
Anew, this loved and scourged of Angels found
Our common brotherhood in sight and sound :
When mellow rang the name Napoleon,
And dim aloft her young Angelical waved.
Between ethereal and gross to choose,
She swung ; her soul desired, her senses craved.
They pricked her dreams, while oft her skies were dun
Behind o'ershadowing foemen : on a tide
They drew the nature having need of pride
Among her fellows for its vital dues :
He seen like some rare treasure-galleon,
Hull down, with masts against the Western hues.

FRANCE

DECEMBER, 1870

NOTE

Written in December, 1870, printed in the *Fortnightly Review*, and published in the volume "Ballads and Poems."

FRANCE

DECEMBER, 1870

I

WE look for her that sunlike stood
Upon the forehead of our day,
An orb of nations, radiating food
For body and for mind alway.
Where is the Shape of glad array ;
The nervous hands, the front of steel,
The clarion tongue ? Where is the bold proud face ?
We see a vacant place ;
We hear an iron heel.

II

O she that made the brave appeal
For manhood when our time was dark,
And from our fetters drove the spark
Which was as lightning to reveal
New seasons, with the swifter play
Of pulses, and benigner day ;

She that divinely shook the dead
From living man ; that stretched ahead
Her resolute forefinger straight,
And marched toward the gloomy gate
Of earth's Untried, gave note, and in
The good name of Humanity
Called forth the daring vision ! she,
She likewise half corrupt of sin,
Angel and Wanton ! can it be ?
Her star has foundered in eclipse,
The shriek of madness on her lips ;
Shreds of her, and no more, we see.
There is horrible convulsion, smothered din,
As of one that in a grave-cloth struggles to be free.

III

Look not for spreading boughs
On the riven forest tree.
Look down where deep in blood and mire
Black thunder plants his feet and ploughs
The soil for ruin : that is France :
Still thrilling like a lyre,
Amazed to shivering discord from a fall
Sudden as that the lurid hosts recall
Who met in heaven the irreparable mischance.
O that is France !
The brilliant eyes to kindle bliss,

The shrewd quick lips to laugh and kiss,
Breasts that a sighing world inspire,
And laughter-dimpled countenance
Where soul and senses caught desire !

IV

Ever invoking fire from heaven, the fire
Has grasped her, unconsumable, but framed
For all the ecstasies of suffering dire.
Mother of Pride, her sanctuary shamed :
Mother of Delicacy, and made a mark
For outrage: Mother of Luxury, stripped stark :
Mother of Heroes, bondsmen : thro' the rains,
Across her boundaries, lo the league-long chains !
Fond Mother of her martial youth ; they pass,
Are spectres in her sight, are mown as grass!
Mother of Honour, and dishonoured : Mother
Of Glory, she condemned to crown with bays
Her victor, and be fountain of his praise.
Is there another curse?   There is another :
Compassionate her madness : is she not
Mother of Reason? she that sees them mown
Like grass, her young ones! Yea, in the low groan
And under the fixed thunder of this hour
Which holds the animate world in one foul blot
Tranced circumambient while relentless Power
Beaks at her heart and claws her limbs down-thrown,

She, with the plunging lightnings overshot,
With madness for an armour against pain,
With milkless breasts for little ones athirst,
And round her all her noblest dying in vain,
Mother of Reason is she, trebly cursed,
To feel, to see, to justify the blow ;
Chamber to chamber of her sequent brain
Gives answer of the cause of her great woe,
Inexorably echoing thro' the vaults,
' 'Tis thus they reap in blood, in blood who sow :
' This is the sum of self-absolvëd faults.'
Doubt not that thro' her grief, with sight supreme,
Thro' her delirium and despair's last dream,
Thro' pride, thro' bright illusion and the brood
Bewildering of her various Motherhood,
The high strong light within her, tho' she bleeds,
Traces the letters of returned misdeeds.
She sees what seed long sown, ripened of late,
Bears this fierce crop ; and she discerns her fate
From origin to agony, and on
As far as the wave washes long and wan
Off one disastrous impulse : for of waves
Our life is, and our deeds are pregnant graves
Blown rolling to the sunset from the dawn.

V

Ah, what a dawn of splendour, when her sowers
Went forth and bent the necks of populations
And of their terrors and humiliations
Wove her the starry wreath that earthward lowers
Now in the figure of a burning yoke!
Her legions traversed North and South and East,
Of triumph they enjoyed the glutton's feast :
They grafted the green sprig, they lopped the oak.
They caught by the beard the tempests, by the scalp
The icy precipices, and clove sheer through
The heart of horror of the pinnacled Alp,
Emerging not as men whom mortals knew.
They were the earthquake and the hurricane,
The lightnings and the locusts, plagues of blight,
Plagues of the revel : they were Deluge rain,
And dreaded Conflagration ; lawless Might.
Death writes a reeling line along the snows,
Where under frozen mists they may be tracked,
Who men and elements provoked to foes,
And Gods : they were of god and beast compact :
Abhorred of all. Yet, how they sucked the teats
Of Carnage, thirsty issue of their dam,
Whose eagles, angrier than their oriflamme,
Flushed the vext earth with blood, green earth forgets.
The gay young generations mask her grief ;
Where bled her children hangs the loaded sheaf.

Forgetful is green earth ; the Gods alone
Remember everlastingly : they strike
Remorselessly, and ever like for like.
By their great memories the Gods are known.

VI

They are with her now, and in her ears, and known.
'Tis they that cast her to the dust for Strength,
Their slave, to feed on her fair body's length,
That once the sweetest and the proudest shone ;
Scoring for hideous dismemberment
Her limbs, as were the anguish-taking breath
Gone out of her in the insufferable descent
From her high chieftainship ; as were she death,
Who hears a voice of justice, feels the knife
Of torture, drinks all ignominy of life.
They are with her, and the painful Gods might weep,
If ever rain of tears came out of heaven
To flatter Weakness and bid Conscience sleep,
Viewing the woe of this Immortal, driven
For the soul's life to drain the maddening cup
Of her own children's blood implacably :
Unsparing even as they to furrow up
The yellow land to likeness of a sea :
The bountiful fair land of vine and grain,
Of wit and grace and ardour, and strong roots,
Fruits perishable, imperishable fruits ;

Furrowed to likeness of the dim grey main
Behind the black obliterating cyclone.

VII

Behold, the Gods are with her, and are known.
Whom they abandon misery persecutes
No more: them half-eyed apathy may loan
The happiness of pitiable brutes.
Whom the just Gods abandon have no light,
No ruthless light of introspective eyes
That in the midst of misery scrutinize
The heart and its iniquities outright.
They rest, they smile and rest; have earned perchance
Of ancient service quiet for a term;
Quiet of old men dropping to the worm;
And so goes out the soul. But not of France.
She cries for grief, and to the Gods she cries,
For fearfully their loosened hands chastize,
And icily they watch the rod's caress
Ravage her flesh from scourges merciless,
But she, inveterate of brain, discerns
That Pity has as little place as Joy
Among their roll of gifts; for Strength she yearns,
For Strength, her idol once, too long her toy.
Lo, Strength is of the plain root-Virtues born:
Strength shall ye gain by service, prove in scorn,
Train by endurance, by devotion shape.

- Strength is not won by miracle or rape.
  It is the offspring of the modest years,
  The gift of sire to son, thro' those firm laws
- Which we name Gods ; which are the righteous cause,
  The cause of man, and manhood's ministers.
  Could France accept the fables of her priests,
  Who blest her banners in this game of beasts,
  And now bid hope that heaven will intercede
  To violate its laws in her sore need,
  She would find comfort in their opiates :
  Mother of Reason ! can she cheat the Fates ?
  Would she, the champion of the open mind,
  The Omnipotent's prime gift—the gift of growth—
  Consent even for a night-time to be blind,
  And sink her soul on the delusive sloth,
  For fruits ethereal and material, both,
  In peril of her place among mankind ?
- The Mother of the many Laughters might
  Call one poor shade of laughter in the light
  Of her unwavering lamp to mark what things
  The world puts faith in, careless of the truth :
  What silly puppet-bodies danced on strings,
  Attached by credence, we appear in sooth,
  Demanding intercession, direct aid,
  When the whole tragic tale hangs on a broken blade !

  She swung the sword for centuries ; in a day
  It slipped her, like a stream cut off from source.

She struck a feeble hand, and tried to pray,
Clamoured of treachery, and had recourse
To drunken outcries in her dream that Force
Needed but hear her shouting to obey.
Was she not formed to conquer? The bright plumes
Of crested vanity shed graceful nods :
Transcendent in her foundries, Arts and looms,
Had France to fear the vengeance of the Gods?
Her faith was on her battle-roll of names
Sheathed in the records of old war ; with dance
And song she thrilled her warriors and her dames,
Embracing her Dishonour : gave him France
From head to foot, France present and to come,
So she might hear the trumpet and the drum—
Bellona and Bacchante ! rushing forth
On yon stout marching Schoolmen of the North.

Inveterate of brain, well knows she why
Strength failed her, faithful to himself the first :
Her dream is done, and she can read the sky,
And she can take into her heart the worst
Calamity to drug the shameful thought.
Of days that made her as the man she served
A name of terror, but a thing unnerved :
Buying the trickster, by the trickster bought,
She for dominion, he to patch a throne.

VIII

Henceforth of her the Gods are known,
Open to them her breast is laid.
Inveterate of brain, heart-valiant,
Never did fairer creature pant
Before the altar and the blade !

IX

Swift fall the blows, and men upbraid,
And friends give echo blunt and cold,
The echo of the forest to the axe.
Within her are the fires that wax
For resurrection from the mould.

X

She snatched at heaven's flame of old,
And kindled nations : she was weak :
Frail sister of her heroic prototype,
The Man ; for sacrifice unripe,
She too must fill a Vulture's beak.
Deride the vanquished, and acclaim
The conqueror, who stains her fame,
Still the Gods love her, for that of high aim
Is this good France, the bleeding thing they stripe.

XI

She shall rise worthier of her prototype
Thro' her abasement deep ; the pain that runs

From nerve to nerve some victory achieves.
They lie like circle-strewn soaked Autumn-leaves
Which stain the forest scarlet, her fair sons!
And of their death her life is: of their blood
From many streams now urging to a flood,
No more divided, France shall rise afresh.
Of them she learns the lesson of the flesh:—
The lesson writ in red since first Time ran
A hunter hunting down the beast in man:
That till the chasing out of its last vice,
The flesh was fashioned but for sacrifice,

Immortal Mother of a mortal host!
Thou suffering of the wounds that will not slay,
Wounds that bring death but take not life away!—
Stand fast and hearken while thy victors boast:
Hearken, and loathe that music evermore.
Slip loose thy garments woven of pride and shame:
The torture lurks in them, with them the blame
Shall pass to leave thee purer than before.
Undo thy jewels, thinking whence they came,
For what, and of the abominable name
Of her who in imperial beauty wore.

O Mother of a fated fleeting host
Conceived in the past days of sin, and born
Heirs of disease and arrogance and scorn,
Surrender, yield the weight of thy great ghost,

F

Like wings on air, to what the heavens proclaim
With trumpets from the multitudinous mounds
Where peace has filled the hearing of thy sons:
Albeit a pang of dissolution rounds
Each new discernment of the undying ones,
Do thou stoop to these graves here scattered wide
Along thy fields, as sunless billows roll;
These ashes have the lesson for the soul.
'Die to thy Vanity, and strain thy Pride,
Strip off thy Luxury: that thou may'st live,
Die to thyself,' they say, 'as we have died
From dear existence and the foe forgive,
Nor pray for aught save in our little space
To warn good seed to greet the fair earth's face.'
O Mother! take their counsel, and so shall
The broader world breathe in on this thy home,
Light clear for thee the counter-changing dome,
Strength give thee, like an ocean's vast expanse
Off mountain cliffs, the generations all,
Not whirling in their narrow rings of foam,
But as a river forward. Soaring France!
Now is Humanity on trial in thee:
Now may'st thou gather humankind in fee:
Now prove that Reason is a quenchless scroll;
Make of calamity thine aureole,
And bleeding head us thro' the troubles of the sea.

ALSACE-LORRAINE

ALSACE-LORRAINE

THE sister Hours in circles linked,
Daughters of men, of men the mates,
Are gone on flow with the day that winked,
With the night that spanned at golden gates.
Mothers, they leave us, quickening seed ;
They bear us grain or flower or weed,
As we have sown ; is nought extinct
For them we fill to be our Fates.
Life of the breath is but the loan ;
Passing death what we have sown.

Pearly are they till the pale inherited stain
Deepens in us, and the mirrors they form on their flow,
Darken to feature and nature : a volumed chain,
Sequent of issue, in various eddies they show.
Theirs is the Book of the River of Life, to read
Leaf by leaf by reapers of long-sown seed :
There doth our shoot up to light from a spiriting sane,

Stand as a tree whereon numberless clusters grow :
Legible there how the heart, with its one false move,
Cast Eurydice pallor on all we love.

Our fervid heart has filled that Book in chief ;
Our fitful heart a wild reflection views ;
Our craving heart of passion suckling grief,
Disowns the author's work it must peruse ;
Inconscient in its leap to wreak the deed,
A round of harvests red from crimson seed,
It marks the current Hours show leaf by leaf,
And rails at Destiny ; nor traces clues ;
Though sometimes it may think what novel light
Will strike their faces when the mind shall write.

II

Succourful daughters of men are the rosed and starred
Revolving Twelves in their fluent germinal rings,
Despite the burden to chasten, abase, depose.
Fallen on France, as the sweep of scythe over sward,
They breathed in her ear their voice of the crystal
　　springs,
That run from a twilight rise, from a twilight close,
Through alternate beams and glooms, rejoicingly
　　young.
Only to Earth's best loved, at the breathless turns
Where Life in fold of the Shadow reclines unstrung,

And a ghostly lamp of their moment's union burns,
Will such pure notes from the fountain-head be sung.

Voice of Earth's very soul to the soul she would see
    renewed :
A song that sought no tears, that laid not a touch on
    the breast
Sobbing aswoon and, like last foxgloves' bells upon
    ferns
In sandy alleys of woodland silence, shedding to bare.
Daughters of Earth and men, they piped of her natural
    brood ;
Her patient helpful four-feet; wings on the flit or in
    nest ;
Paws at our old-world task to scoop a defensive lair ;
Snouts at hunt through the scented grasses ; en-
    havened scuts
Flashing escape under show of a laugh nigh the
    mossed burrow-mouth.
Sack-like droop bronze pears on the nailed branch-
    frontage of huts,
To greet those wedded toilers from acres where sweat
    is a shower.
Snake, cicada, lizard, on lavender slopes up South,
Pant for joy of a sunlight driving the fielders to bower.
Sharpened in silver by one chance breeze is the olive's
    grey ;
A royal-mantle floats, a red fritillary hies ;

The bee, for whom no flower of garden or wild has
    nay,
Noises, heard if but named, so hot is the trade he plies.
Processions beneath green arches of herbage, the long
    colonnades ;
Laboured mounds that a foot or a wanton stick may
    subvert ;
Homely are they for a lowly look on bedewed grass-
    blades,
On citied fir-droppings, on twisted wreaths of the
    worm in dirt.

Does naught so loosen our sight from the despot
    heart, to receive
Balm of a sound Earth's primary heart at its active
    beat :
The motive, yet servant of energy ; simple as morn
    and eve ;
Treasureless, fetterless ; free of the bonds of a great
    conceit :
Unwounded even by cruel blows on a body that
    writhes ;
Nor whimpering under misfortune ; elusive of ob-
    stacles ; prompt
To quit any threatened familiar domain seen doomed
    by the scythes ;
Its day's hard business done, the score to the good
    accompt.

Creatures of forest and mead, Earth's essays in being,
all kinds
Bound by the navel-knot to the Mother, never astray,
They in the ear upon ground will pour their intuitive
minds,
Cut man's tangles for Earth's first broad rectilinear
way :
Admonishing loftier reaches, the rich adventurous
shoots,
Pushes of tentative curves, embryonic upwreathings
in air ;
Not always the sprouts of Earth's root-Laws preserv-
ing her brutes ;
Oft but our primitive hungers licentious in fine and
fair.

Yet the like aërial growths may chance be the deli-
cate sprays,
Infant of Earth's most urgent in sap, her fierier zeal
For entry on Life's upper fields : and soul thus flour-
ishing pays
The martyr's penance, mark for brutish in man to
heel.

Her, from a nerveless well among stagnant pools of
the dry,
Through her good aim at divine, shall commune with
Earth remake ;

Fraternal unto sororial, her, where abashed she may
lie,
Divinest of man shall clasp; a world out of darkness
awake,
As it were with the Resurrection's eyelids uplifted,
to see
Honour in shame, in substance the spirit, in that dry
fount
Jets of the songful ascending silvery-bright water-
tree
Spout, with our Earth's unbaffled resurgent desire for
the mount,
Though broken at intervals, clipped, and barren in
seeming it be.

For this at our nature arises rejuvenescent from Earth,
However respersive the blow and nigh on infernal the
fall,
The chastisement drawn down on us merited : are we
of worth
Amid our satanic excrescences, this, for the less than
a call,
Will Earth reprime, man cherish; the God who is in
us and round,
Consenting, the God there seen. Impiety speaks despair ;
Religion the virtue of serving as things of the furrowy
ground,

Debtors for breath while breath with our fellows in
    service we share.
Not such of the crowned discrowned
Can Earth or humanity spare ;
Such not the God let die.

III

Eastward of Paris morn is high ;
And darkness on that Eastward side
The heart of France beholds : a thorn
Is in her frame where shines the morn :
A rigid wave usurps her sky,
With eagle crest and eagle-eyed
To scan what wormy wrinkles hint
Her forces gathering : she the thrown
From station, lopped of an arm, astounded, lone,
Reading late History as a foul misprint :
Imperial, Angelical,
At strife commingled in her frame convulsed ;
Shame of her broken sword, a ravening gall ;
Pain of the limb where once her warm blood pulsed ;
These tortures to distract her underneath
Her whelmed Aurora's shade. But in that space
When lay she dumb beside her trampled wreath,
Like an unburied body mid the tombs,
Feeling against her heart life's bitter probe
For life, she saw how children of her race,

The many sober sons and daughters, plied,
By cottage lamplight through the water-globe,
By simmering stew-pots, by the serious looms,
Afield, in factories, with the birds astir,
Their nimble feet and fingers ; not denied
Refreshful chatter, laughter, galliard songs.
So like Earth's indestructible they were,
That wrestling with its anguish rose her pride,
To feel where in each breast the thought of her,
On whom the circle Hours laid leaded thongs,
Was constant ; spoken sometimes in low tone
At lip or in a fluttered look,
A shortened breath : and they were her loved own ;
Nor ever did they waste their strength with tears,
For pity of the weeper, nor rebuke,
Though mainly they were charged to pay her debt,
The Mother having conscience in arrears ;
Ready to gush the flood of vain regret,
Else hearken to her weaponed children's moan
Of stifled rage invoking vengeance : hell's,
If heaven should fail the counter-wave that swells
In blood and brain for retribution swift.
Those helped not : wings to her soul were these who
        yet
Could welcome day for labour, night for rest,
Enrich her treasury, built of cheerful thrift,
Of honest heart, beyond all miracles ;
And likened to Earth's humblest were Earth's best.

IV

Brooding on her deep fall, the many strings
Which formed her nature set a thought on Kings,
As aids that might the low-laid cripple lift ;
And one among them hummed devoutly leal,
While passed the sighing breeze along her breast.
Of Kings by the festive vanquishers rammed down
Her gorge since fell the Chief, she knew their crown ;
Upon her through long seasons was its grasp,
For neither soul's nor body's weal ;
As much bestows the robber wasp,
That in the hanging apple makes a meal,
And carves a face of abscess where was fruit
Ripe ruddy. They would blot
Her radiant leap above the slopes acute,
Off summit to celestial ; impute
The wanton's aim to her divinest shot ;
Bid her walk History backward over gaps ;
Abhor the day of Phrygian caps ;
Abjure her guerdon, execrate herself ;
The Hapsburg, Hohenzollern, Guelph,
Admire repentant ; reverently prostrate
Her person unto the belly-god ; of whom
Is inward plenty and external bloom ;
Enough of pomp and state
And carnival to quench

The breast's desires of an intemperate wench,
The head's ideas beyond legitimate.

She flung them : she was France : nor with far frown
Her lover from the embrace of her refrained :
But in her voice an interwoven wire,
The exultation of her gross renown,
Struck deafness at her heavens, and they waned
Over a look ill-gifted to aspire.

Wherefore, as an abandonment, irate,
The intemperate summoned up her trumpet days,
Her treasure-galleon's wondrous freight.
The cannon-name she sang and shrieked ; transferred
Her soul's allegiance ; o'er the Tyrant slurred,
Tranced with the zeal of her first fawning gaze,
To clasp his trophy flags and hail him Saint.

V

She hailed him Saint :
And her Jeanne unsainted, foully sung !
The virgin who conceived a France when funeral
    glooms
Across a land aquake with sharp disseverance hung :
Conceived, and under stress of battle brought her
    forth ;
Crowned her in purification of feud and foeman's taint ;

Taught her to feel her blood her being, know her
    worth,
Have joy of unity : the Jeanne bescreeched, bescoffed,
Who flamed to ashes, flew up wreaths of faggot fumes ;
Through centuries a star in vapour-folds aloft.

For her people to hail her Saint,
Were no lifting of her, Earth's gem,
Earth's chosen, Earth's throb on divine :
In the ranks of the starred she is one,
While man has thought on our line :
No lifting of her, but for them,
Breath of the mountain, beam of the sun
Through mist, out of swamp-fires' lures release,
Youth on the forehead, the rough right way
Seen to be footed : for them the heart's peace,
By the mind's war won for a permanent miracle day.

Her arms below her sword-hilt crossed,
The heart of that high-hallowed Jeanne
Into the furnace-pit she tossed
Before her body knew the flame,
And sucked its essence : warmth for righteous work,
An undivided power to speed her aim.
She had no self but France : the sainted man
No France but self. Him warrior and clerk,
Free of his iron clutch ; and him her young,
In whirled imagination mastodonized ;

And him her penmen, him her poets ; all
For the visioned treasure-galleon astrain ;
Sent zenithward on bass and treble tongue,
Till solely through his glory France was prized.
She who had her Jeanne ;
The child of her industrious ;
Earth's truest, earth's pure fount from the main ;
And she who had her one day's mate,
In the soul's view illustrious
Past blazonry, her Immaculate ;
Those hours of slavish Empire would recall ;
Thrill to the rattling anchor-chain
She heard upon a day in " I who can " ;
Start to the softened, tremulous bugle-blare
Of that Caesarean Italian
Across the storied fields of trampled grain,
As to a Vercingetorix of old Gaul
Blowing the rally against a Caesar's reign.
Her soul's protesting sobs she drowned to swear
Fidelity unto the sainted man,
Whose nimbus was her crown ; and be again
The foreigner in Europe, known of none,
None knowing ; sight to dazzle, voice to stun.
Rearward she stepped, with thirst for Europe's van ;
The dream she nursed a snare,
The flag she bore a pall.

VI

In Nature is no rearward step allowed.
Hard on the rock Reality do we dash
To be shattered, if the material dream propels.
The worship to departed splendour vowed,
Conjured a simulacrum, wove her lash,
For the slow measure timed her peal of bells.

Thereof was the cannon-name a mockery round her
    hills ;
For the will of wills,
Its flaccid ape,
Weak as the final echo off a giant's bawl :
Napoleon for disdain,
His banner steeped in crape.
Thereof the barrier of Alsace-Lorraine ;
The frozen billow crested to its fall ;
Dismemberment ; disfigurement ;
Her history blotted ; her proud mantle rent ;
And ever that one word to reperuse,
With eyes behind a veil of fiery dews ;
Knelling the spot where Gallic soil defiled,
Showed her sons' valour as a frenzied child
In arms of the mailed man.
Word that her mind must bear, her heart put under
    ban,
Lest burst it : unto her eyes a ghost,

G

Incredible though manifest: a scene
Stamped with her new Saint's name: and all his
    host
A wattled flock the foeman's dogs between!

VII

Mark where a credible ghost pulls bridle to view that
    bare
Corpse of a field still reddening cloud, and alive in its
    throes
Beneath her Purgatorial Saint's evocative stare:
Brand on his name, the gulf of his glory, his Legend's
    close.
A lustreless Phosphor heading for daybeam Night's
    dead-born,
His underworld eyeballs grip the cast of the land for
    a fray
Expugnant; swift up the heights, with the Victor's
    instinctive scorn
Of the trapped below, he rides; he beholds, and a
    two-fold grey,
Even as the misty sun growing moon that a frost
    enrings,
Is shroud on the shrouded; he knows him there in
    the helmeted ranks.
The golden eagles flap lame wings,
The black double-headed are round their flanks.

He is there in midst of the pupils he harried to
brain-awake, trod into union ; lo,

These are his Epic's tutored Dardans, yon that Rhap-
sode's Achaeans to know.

Nor is aught of an equipollent conflict seen, nor the
weaker's flashed device ;

Headless is offered a breast to beaks deliberate, for-
mal, assured, precise.

Ruled by the mathematician's hand, they solve their
problem, as on a slate.

This is the ground foremarked, and the day ; their
leader modestly hazarded date.

His helmeted ranks might be draggers of pools or
reapers of plains for the warrior's guile

Displayed ; they haul, they rend, as in some orderly
office mercantile.

And a timed artillery speaks full-mouthed on a stut-
tering feeble reduced to naught.

Can it be France, an army of France, tricked, netted,
convulsive, all writhen caught ?

Arterial blood of an army's heart outpoured, the Grey
Observer sees :

A forest of France in thunder comes, like a landslide
hurled off her Pyrenees.

Torrent and forest ramp, roll, sling on for a charge
against iron, reason, Fate ;

It is gapped through the mass midway, bare ribs and
    dust ere the helmeted feel its weight.
So the blue billow white - plumed is plunged upon
    shingle to screaming withdrawal, but snatched,
Waved is the laurel eternal yielded by Death o'er the
    waste of brave men outmatched.
The France of the fury was there, the thing he had
    wielded, whose honour was dearer than life;
The Prussia despised, the harried, the trodden, was
    here; his pupil, the scholar in strife.

He haled to heel, in a spasm of will,
From sleep or debate, a mannikin squire
With head of a merlin hawk and quill
Acrow on an ear. At him rained fire
From a blast of eyeballs hotter than speech,
To say what a deadly poison stuffed
The France here laid in her bloody ditch,
Through the Legend passing human puffed.

Credible ghost of the field which from him descends,
Each dark anniversary day will its father return,
Haling his shadow to spy where the Legend ends,
That penman trumpeter's part in the wreck discern.

There, with the cup it presents at her lips, she stands,
France, with her future staked on the word it may
    pledge.

The vengeance urged of desire a reserve counter-
    mands ;
The patience clasped totters hard on the precipice-
    edge.

Lopped of an arm, mother love for her own springs
    quick,
To curdle the milk in her breasts for the young they
    feed,
At thought of her single hand, and the lost so nigh.
Mother love for her own, who raised her when she lay
    sick
Nigh death, and would in like fountains fruitlessly
    bleed,
Withholds the fling of her heart on the further die.

Of love is wisdom. Is it great love, then wise
Will our wild heart be, though whipped unto madness
    more
By its mentor's counselling voice than thoughtfully
    reined.
Desire of the wave for the shore,
Passion for one last agony under skies,
To make her heavens remorseful, she restrained.

VIII

On her lost arm love bade her look ;
On her one hand to meditate ;
The tumult of her blood abate ;

Disaster face, derision brook :
Forbade the page of her Historic Muse,
Until her demon his last hold forsook,
And smoothly, with no countenance of hate,
Her conqueror she could scan to measure. Thence
The strange new Winter stream of ruling sense,
Cold, comfortless, but braced to disabuse,
Ran through the mind of this most lowly laid ;
From the top billow of victorious War,
Down in the flagless troughs at ebb and flow ;
A wreck ; her past, her future, both in shade.

She read the things that are ;
Reality unaccepted read
For sign of the distraught, and took her blow
To brain ; herself read through ;
Wherefore her predatory Glory paid
Napoleon ransom knew.
Her nature's many strings hot gusts did jar
Against the note of reason uttered low,
Ere passionate with duty she might wed,
Compel the bride's embrace of her stern groom.
Joined at an altar liker to the tomb,
Nest of the Furies their first nuptial bed,
They not the less were mated and proclaimed
The rational their issue. Then she rose.

See how the rush of southern Springtide glows
Oceanic in the chariot-wheel's ascent,

Illuminated with one breath. The maimed,
Torn, tortured, winter-visaged, suddenly
Had stature; to the world's wonderment,
Fair features, grace of mien, nor least
The comic dimples round her April mouth,
Sprung of her intimate humanity.
She stood before mankind the very South
Rapt out of frost to flowery drapery;
Unshadowed save when somewhiles she looked East.

IX

Let but the rational prevail,
Our footing is on ground though all else fail:
Our kiss of Earth is then a plight
To walk within her Laws and have her light.
Choice of the life or death lies in ourselves;
There is no fate but when unreason lours.
This Land the cheerful toiler delves,
The thinker brightens with fine wit,
The lovelier grace as lyric flowers,
Those rosed and starred revolving Twelves
Shall nurse for effort infinite
While leashed to brain the heart of France the Fair
Beats tempered music and its lead subserves.
Washed from her eyes the Napoleonic glare,
Divinely raised by that in her divine,
Not the clear sight of Earth's blunt actual swerves

When her lost look, as on a wave of wine,
Rolls Eastward, and the mother-flag descries
Caress with folds and curves
The fortress over Rhine,
Beneath the one tall spire.
Despite her brooding thought, her nightlong sighs,
Her anguish in desire,
She sees, above the brutish paw
Alert on her still quivering limb—
As little in past time she saw,
Nor when dispieced as prey,
As victrix when abhorred—
A Grand Germania, stout on soil;
Audacious up the ethereal dim;
The forest's Infant; the strong hand for toil;
The patient brain in twilights when astray;
Shrewdest of heads to foil and counterfoil;
The sceptic and devout; the potent sword;
With will and armed to help in hewing way
For Europe's march; and of the most golden chord
Of the Heliconian lyre
Excellent mistress. Yea, she sees, and can admire;
Still seeing in what walks the Gallia leads;
And with what shield upon Alsace-Lorraine
Her wary sister's doubtful look misreads
A mother's throbs for her lost: so loved: so near:
Magnetic. Hard the course for her to steer,
The leap against the sharpened spikes restrain.

For the belted Overshadower hard the course,
On whom devolves the spirit's touchstone, Force :
Which is the strenuous arm, to strike inclined,
That too much adamantine makes the mind ;
Forgets it coin of Nature's rich Exchange ;
Contracts horizons within present sight :
Amalekite to-day, across its range
Indisputable ; to-morrow Simeonite.

X

The mother who gave birth to Jeanne ;
Who to her young Angelical sprang ;
Who lay with Earth and heard the notes she sang,
And heard her truest sing them ; she may reach
Heights yet unknown of nations ; haply teach
A thirsting world to learn 'tis " she who can."

She that in History's Heliaea pleads
The nation flowering conscience o'er the beast ;
With heart expurged of rancour, tame of greeds ;
With the winged mind from fang and claw released ;—
Will such a land be seen ?   It will be seen ;—
Shall stand adjudged our foremost and Earth's Queen.
Acknowledgment that she of God proceeds
The invisible makes visible, as his priest,
To her is yielded by a world reclaimed.
And stands she mutilated, fancy-shamed,

Yet strong in arms, yet strong in self-control,
Known valiant, her maternal throbs repressed,
Discarding vengeance, Giant with a soul ;—
My faith in her when she lay low
Was fountain ; now as wave at flow
Beneath the lights, my faith in God is best ;—
On France has come the test
Of what she holds within
Responsive to Life's deeper springs.
She above the nations blest
In fruitful and in liveliest,
In all that servant earth to heavenly bidding brings,
The devotee of Glory, she may win
Glory despoiling none, enrich her kind,
Illume her land, and take the royal seat
Unto the strong self-conqueror assigned.

But ah, when speaks a loaded breath the double name,
Humanity's old Foeman winks agrin.
Her constant Angel eyes her heart's quick beat,
The thrill of shadow coursing through her frame,
Like wind among the ranks of amber wheat.
Our Europe, vowed to unity or torn,
Observes her face, as shepherds note the morn,
And in a ruddy beacon mark an end
That for the flock in their grave hearing rings.
Specked overhead the imminent vulture wings
At poise, one fatal movement indiscreet,

Sprung from the Ætna passions' mad revolts,
Draws down ; the midnight hovers to descend ;
And dire as Indian noons of ulcer heat
Anticipating tempest and the bolts,
Hangs curtained terrors round our next day's door,
Death's emblems for the breast of Europe flings ;
The breast that waits a spark to fire her store.
Shall, then, the great vitality, France,
Signal the backward step once more ;
Again a Goddess Fortune trace
Amid the Deities, and pledge to chance
One whom we never could replace ?
Now may she tune her nature's many strings
To noble harmony, be seen, be known.

It was the foreign France, the unruly, feared ;
Little for all her witcheries endeared ;
Theatrical of arrogance, a sprite
With gaseous vapours overblown,
In her conceit of power ensphered,
Foredoomed to violate and atone ;
Her the grim conqueror's iron might
Avengeing clutched, distrusting rent ;
Not that sharp intellect with fire endowed
To cleave our webs, run lightnings through our cloud ;
Not virtual France, the France benevolent,
The chivalrous, the many-stringed, sublime
At intervals, and oft in sweetest chime ;

Though perilously instrument,
A breast for any having godlike gleam.
This France could no antagonist disesteem,
To spurn at heel and confiscate her brood.
Albeit a waverer between heart and mind,
And laurels won from sky or plucked from blood,
Which wither all the wreath when intertwined,
This cherishable France she may redeem.
Beloved of Earth, her heart should feel at length
How much unto Earth's offspring it doth owe.
Obstructions are for levelling, have we strength ;
'Tis poverty of soul conceives a foe.
Rejected be the wrath that keeps unhealed
Her panting wound ; to higher Courts appealed
The wrongs discerned of higher : Europe waits :
She chooses God or gambles with the Fates.
Shines the new Helen in Alsace-Lorraine,
A darker river severs Rhine and Rhone,
Is heard a deadlier Epic of the twain ;
We see a Paris burn
Or France Napoleon.

For yet he breathes whom less her heart forswears
While trembles its desire to thwart her mind :
The Tyrant lives in Victory's return.
What figure with recurrent footstep fares
Around those memoried tracks of scarlet mud,
To sow her future from an ashen urn

By lantern-light, as dragons' teeth are sown?
Of bleeding pride the piercing seër is blind.
But, cleared her eyes of that ensanguined scud
Distorting her true features, to be shown
Benignly luminous, one who bears
Humanity at breast, and she might learn
How surely the excelling generous find
Renouncement is possession. Sure
As light enkindles light when heavenly earthly mates,
The flame of pure immits the flame of pure,
Magnanimous magnanimous creates.
So to majestic beauty stricken rears
Hard-visaged rock against the risen glow;
And men are in the secret with the spheres,
Whose glory is celestially to bestow.

Now nation looks to nation, that may live
Their common nurseling, like the torrent's flower,
Shaken by foul Destruction's fast-piled heap.
On France is laid the proud initiative
Of sacrifice in one self-mastering hour,
Whereby more than her lost one will she reap;
Perchance the very lost regain,
To count it less than her superb reward.
Our Europe, where is debtor each to each,
Pass measure of excess, and war is Cain,
Fraternal from the Seaman's beach,
From answering Rhine in grand accord,

From Neva beneath Northern cloud,
And from our Transatlantic Europe loud,
Will hail the rare example for their theme ;
Give response, as rich foliage to the breeze ;
In their entrusted nurseling know them one :
Like a brave vessel under press of steam,
Abreast the winds and tides, on angry seas,
Plucked by the heavens forlorn of present sun,
Will drive through darkness, and with faith supreme,
Have sight of haven and the crowded quays.

Butler & Tanner, The Selwood Printing Works, Frome, and London.